*Serenade* by Don Maitz.

*Above:* Actors dressed as a Chinese zombie and vampire. In China, the *jiangshi,* or hopping vampires, are feared. The jiangshi suck the "life-force" out of their victims.

In Mexico, evil creatures known as the "goat suckers," or *el chupacabra,* are said to drink the blood of goats and other animals. These bloodsuckers may be a type of animal, an undead spirit, or a race of small humanoids.

In the late 1840s, Ireland suffered a terrible famine. Blight destroyed most potatoes, one of the main crops in Ireland. Hundreds of thousands of people starved. Some were forced to drink the blood of farm animals to survive. After the potato famine, stories arose about the *fir gorta* (the "man of hunger"). The part-human, part-spirit beast grew to like the taste of blood, and prowled around the countryside searching for fresh victims.

Scotland is the home of blood-drinking fairies called *glaistigs.* They take the form of beautiful women. Men are unable to resist their call, but pay a terrible price: the glaistigs lure them into swamps and drink their blood.

In Iceland, people who live too close to cemeteries are afraid of the *aptrgangr.* The word aptrgangr means "one who walks after death." These creatures have immense strength. The aptrgangr devours its victims, or drinks their blood. Then the victim becomes an aptrgangr. The only way to deal with an aptrgangr is to wrestle it and win, and then force it back into its grave.

*Above:* A lighted graveyard in Vesttmannaeyjar, Iceland. In this area, people fear the *aptrgangr,* a strong, vampire-like being that drinks its victims' blood. An aptrgangr must be wrestled and forced back to its grave.

Some of the stranger types of vampire-like creatures are the *jiangshi,* the dreaded hopping vampires of China. Originally, they did not drink blood, but sucked the "life-force" out of their victims. The jiangshi were people who did not get a proper burial in their hometown. But because they were dead, they couldn't move, so they had to hop back to their hometown to get a proper burial.

The *churels* emerged in stories from India. Churels were women who had died in childbirth, and had come back to drink the blood of the living. They frequently appeared as beautiful women, wearing a hooded gown and carrying a lantern. They lurked in cemeteries hoping to draw innocent victims to their doom.

# THE REAL DRACULA

There really was a person named Dracula. He was a prince who ruled a land called Walachia. Both Walachia (where the real Dracula is from) and Transylvania (where Bram Stoker's character is from) are today within the country of Romania, in Eastern Europe.

Dracula ruled in the late 1400s. His given name was Vlad, sometimes called Vlad III (his father, Vlad II, reigned before him). The Church gave his father the title of *Dracul,* which meant "dragon." He received this honor because he was valiant in defending the land from armies of the Turkish Ottoman Empire. When Vlad III took over, he adopted the name *Dracula,* which means *Son of Dracul.*

Only oral tradition describes Dracula's brutal rule, so it is difficult to separate the stories told about him from the actual facts of his reign. It seems that Vlad Dracula was successful in defending his homeland from the Ottoman Empire. This may have been due, in part, to the ferociously brutal way in which he dealt with his enemies. He was given the name *Vlad the Impaler* because he executed enemies by impaling them on large stakes set in the ground. His enemies included not only the Turks, but also anyone who committed a crime, or anyone who showed him the slightest amount of disrespect.

Vlad was a savage ruler. He tortured and killed thousands of foreigners and fellow Walachians, but there are no stories about him actually drinking blood. However, in 1897, when Bram Stoker wrote his novel *Dracula,* he used Vlad Dracula as the main inspiration of the story, due to Vlad's bloodthirsty reputation.

Vlad Dracula died about 1476. Historians are unsure how he died. One story says family members assassinated him; another story says he died in battle, perhaps killed by his own troops. His final resting place also remains a mystery.

*Facing Page:* Vlad Dracula. He was given the name *Vlad the Impaler* because he impaled his enemies on large stakes set in the ground.

# REAL VAMPIRES?

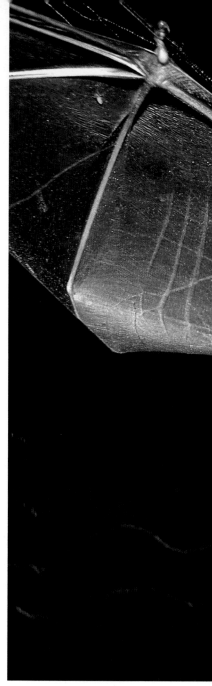

As late as the 17th and 18th centuries, many people in Europe and the Americas believed in vampires. Sometimes they actually dug up people's graves to find out if the bodies were still in their coffins. The living wanted to make sure that the dead weren't making nightly visits to the necks of the living. Unfortunately, this grave digging probably only made vampire-mania worse. When dead bodies decompose, their lips and gums recede, revealing long and ugly teeth. So, when people dug up bodies, they saw corpses with long, gnarly fangs, which may have been mistaken for undead vampires.

While there is no actual vampire disease, there are some medical conditions that perhaps started the vampire folklore, or perhaps reinforced it. There is a rare genetic disease called *cutaneous porphyria*. This disease makes people very sensitive to sunlight. When exposed to the sun, their skin will blister, swell up, or get red. In fact, these people can get a sunburn on a cloudy day. There is no cure for this disease, and so people with this condition must avoid sunlight, only coming out at night.

*Below:* A person with the rare disease cutaneous porphyria.

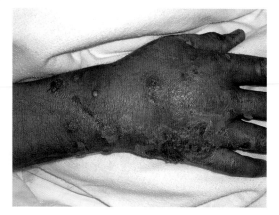

In the Unites States, rabies is a very rare disease. Only a few people contract the disease each year. People get rabies when a rabid animal bites them. Today, we have medicines that can cure and prevent rabies, but throughout most of history, rabies was a big concern. Most of the people who were bitten by rabid animals ended up getting rabies and dying. People with rabies become confused, convulse, and have hallucinations, seeing things that aren't there.

*Above:* A vampire bat trapped in a net in Brazil in 2005. It was tested for rabies, a disease that has spread across the region.

One of the symptoms of rabies includes frothing at the mouth. Rabies victims have too much saliva. They also have difficulty swallowing, so a watery froth can appear on their lips. This froth can sometimes appear red and bloody. It may have looked like they had just feasted on blood. Perhaps some of the vampire folklore comes from people who were suffering from rabies.

What if someone had cutaneous porphyria and a severe allergy to garlic? Would people think that person was a vampire? What if someone was bitten by a rabid vampire bat, and he or she were seen with red foam on their lips? Would people accuse that person of vampirism? Before modern times, superstitious people saw conditions like this and thought, "This proves that vampires exist." Sometimes, when we think something exists, we find the evidence to prove our own beliefs.

*Right:* A young girl wears a necklace of garlic. It was believed that garlic would keep vampires away.

*Above:* An actor plays a modern-day vampire.

# VAMPIRE MOVIES

**V**ampires have been a favorite subject of filmmakers since movies first became popular in the beginning of the 20$^{th}$ century. Vampires have frightened audiences worldwide, from Hollywood to Mexico, and from Germany to China. Following are only a few highlights of famous vampire films:

*Above:* Orlok, the killer vampire, stands aboard a ship in the 1922 German silent film *Nosferatu.*

*Nosferatu* (1922). The story line of this German-made silent movie follows Bram Stoker's novel very closely, until the end of

*Above:* A scene from the 1922 silent film *Nosferatu,* starring Max Schreck as Count Orlok, the sinister vampire.

the film. A businessman named Hutter travels to Transylvania to work on a real-estate deal with the reclusive Count Orlok, who lives in a remote castle deep in the wilderness. Hutter eventually realizes that his sinister host is a vampire. After several creepy encounters, the businessman is imprisoned inside the castle by the count. Hutter watches helplessly as Orlok is loaded into a coffin, which is transported by ship to the German port city of Bremen. When the ship lands, the townspeople discover that the entire crew is dead. A terrible plague soon grips Bremen. The vampire is the source of the evil scourge, and the town appears helpless to stop it. Meanwhile, Hutter finally escapes from the castle, then reunites with his wife, Ellen. They go on a quest to kill Count Orlok. Ellen tricks Orlok into staying out until the sun comes up, giving her own life to kill the vampire.

*Above:* Bela Lugosi became famous for his powerful performance as Count Dracula.

*Above:* A poster from 1931's *Dracula,* starring Bela Lugosi and Helen Chandler.

*Dracula* (1931). This movie also closely follows Bram Stoker's novel. Making the movie was a big gamble for the film company, Universal Studios. The original actors that the studio wanted were unavailable, and the Great Depression was severely hurting the nation's economy at the time. The studio didn't know if people would spend their hard-earned money on entertainment. Furthermore, even though Stoker's novel had been very popular, the studio was unsure if the movie-going public was ready for a full-length horror film about a blood-sucking vampire. Eventually, Universal picked Hungarian-born actor Bela Lugosi to play Count Dracula. He brought a powerful presence and a terrifying richness to the role. Before the movie was released, the studio started a rumor that the movie was so scary that people had fainted in the theater. Consequently, people jammed into theaters to see the movie, making it a big success.

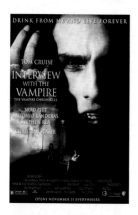

*Interview with the Vampire* (1994). This movie portrays an actual interview with Louis, a vampire played by Brad Pitt, who describes the boredom of immortality and the horror of being a vampire. His story begins in the 1790s, when Louis' wife and child die. Louis, in despair at the loss, meets up with Lestat de Lioncourt, a vampire played by Tom Cruise. Lioncourt gives him a choice: death or immortality as a vampire. Louis chooses to become a vampire.

*Underworld* (2003). In this film, vampires and werewolves have been involved in a centuries-old war, all beneath the notice of humans. Kate Beckinsale plays Selene, a "death dealer," one of the vampire warriors trained to kill werewolves. The werewolves try to kidnap a human in order to create a werewolf-vampire hybrid, a creature that would have the strengths of both but the weaknesses of neither. As the movie unfolds, Selene realizes that not everything is as it appears to be. *Underworld* was so popular the studio made a 2006 sequel, titled *Underworld: Evolution.*

*Blade* (1998). Wesley Snipes plays Blade, a vampire hunter who is himself half human and half undead. In the film, vampires have always secretly lived alongside humanity. The main villain is a vampire named Frost, who no longer wants to hide, but instead wants to enslave humanity. To stop Frost's plan, Blade has help from two humans. His partner creates special weapons, and a doctor helps him with the medicines he needs to keep him from turning completely into a vampire. *Blade* spawned two sequels, *Blade II* in 2002, and *Blade Trinity* in 2004.

*Van Helsing* (2004). In this film, Dracula has been having children with his vampire wives, but children of the undead are born dead. So, Dracula has to use the scientific knowledge of Dr. Victor Frankenstein to try to reanimate his children—to bring them to life. Hugh Jackman plays Van Helsing, an adventurer who must protect other monster hunters and stop Dracula from bringing thousands of vampire children back to life.

*Sometimes After Sunset*
by Don Maitz.

# GLOSSARY

**FOLKLORE**

The unwritten traditions, legends, and customs of a culture. Folklore is usually passed down by word of mouth from generation to generation.

**GREAT DEPRESSION**

A time in American history, beginning in 1929 and lasting for several years, when the stock market crashed, which resulted in business failures across the country and the loss of jobs for millions of people.

**HALLUCINATION**

The perception of a sight or sound that isn't actually there. Hallucinations can occur because of mental illness, or be induced by certain medicines. Druids and witches used medicines to bring on hallucinations in order to contact what they believed to be the spirit world.

**HOLY WATER**

Water blessed by a priest, used for spiritual cleansing and purification.

**PLAGUE**

A disease that spreads easily and rapidly through a populated area, often resulting in a large number of deaths. Sufferers experience fever and delirium. A major outbreak occurred in London, England, in 1665-1666, spread by fleas on the city's rats, although many thought the disease was caused by the rodents themselves. Known as The Great Plague, between 75,000-100,000 people died, nearly a fifth of the city's population.

**RABID**

An animal or human being is said to be rabid when they have the disease rabies. Rabies is a disease caused by a virus that affects the central nervous system (brain and spinal cord) of mammals, including humans. Rabies causes excessive saliva, abnormal behavior, and eventual paralysis and death. People can be exposed to rabies when bitten by an infected wild or domestic animal.

**ROMANIA**

A country in the southeastern part of Central Europe, roughly the size of Oregon.

### TRANCE
A kind of hypnotic mental state. A person in a trance doesn't seem to be affected by interruptions from the outside world. Instead, he seems to be intensely concentrating on something, sometimes chanting phrases over and over.

### TRANSYLVANIA
A region of Romania bordered on one side by the Transylvanian Alps, and on the other by the Carpathian Mountains. After Bram Stoker wrote *Dracula*, it became famous as a country filled with vampires.

### UNDEAD
A reanimated body of a dead person. A part of stories and legends in many cultures, the undead appear in different forms such as ghosts, vampires, or zombies.

*Above:* Willem Dafoe in a scene from 2000's *Shadow of the Vampire*. Dafoe is shown playing Max Schreck, the actor in the original 1922 *Nosferatu* film.

# INDEX

*Above:* A poster from 1931's *Dracula.*